Underneath the Poetry with Her Diary

r. A. bentinck

IyaPublishing
$5 South Turkeyen,
Georgetown, Guyana.

fypublishing@gmail.com

Her Diary / r. A. bentinck

Dedication

To those who have survived and those who will

"An abuser isn't abusive 24/7. They usually demonstrate positive character traits most of the time. That's what makes the abuse so confusing when it happens, and what makes leaving so much more difficult." *-Miya Yamanouchi*

Contents

Author's Preface

There are some stories people whisper. Some they bury. And some live through quietly, hoping no one ever finds out.

This collection was born from the kinds of stories women told me in moments when their voices trembled, or their hands shook, or their eyes tried to hold back memories too heavy to say out loud. These were not dramatic confessions meant for applause. They were private truths, shared in fragments, in metaphors, in passing sentences that revealed more than they intended.

For years I carried those fragments: -the bruised silences, -the rehearsed excuses, -the unspoken fears, -the secret hopes.

I never set out to become the keeper of these stories. But somehow, I became the person women trusted to hold what they could not carry alone. Their truths stayed with me. Their pain stayed with me. Their courage stayed with me. Eventually, I realized that silence does not protect the wounded. It protects the wound.

So, I chose to write. Not to expose them. Not to sensationalize their suffering. Not to claim their experiences as my own. But to honor the women who survived what should have broken them.

This book is a collection of poems inspired by the truths behind closed doors. Truths wrapped in diary entries, half-smiles, apologies, and scars no one ever sees. These pages explore the emotional landscapes of love, fear, betrayal, hope, and the long walk back to oneself. They are stitched together from the echoes of real lives, but written with the sensitivity and respect those lives deserve.

If you find yourself somewhere in these pages, it is not because your story has been stolen. It is because your story is not as isolated as you were made to believe.

To every woman who ever whispered "I'm fine" while drowning inside. To every daughter who learned to hide her wounds. To every partner who stayed too long. To every survivor who walked away and rebuilt herself from dust.

These poems are for you.

I hope they resonate. I hope they remind you that you are not alone. I hope they help you release the weight you've been carrying in silence. And most of all, I hope they inspire you to turn the page.

Because somewhere in this collection, you might discover the sentence, the stanza, or the truth you've been waiting years to hear.

Turn the page. Her diary is open now.

HER OPENED DIARY

Secrets Revealed

Blinded by Love

i didn't see
this coming
i didn't see
this in him

where did it come from?
why does he hit me so hard?

i'm not skilled enough
to be in this boxing ring,

and he doesn't seem

to care that i don't have on
any gloves.

i am not punching back.

he is relentless in
his mindless attacks.

I will Fight for This Love

i have come too far

to turn back now,

i have given up too much

to let go now.

i am going

to fight for

what is mine

i'm not giving up

on this love.

one songwriter says

it hurts to be in love,

so i'm prepared

tu endure the pains.

Bruised

i'm starting to think

i was a camouflage

abuse specimen.

black and blue

patterns

all over

my body

some in

unspeakable places.

Bitch Slapped

he said

he had to

bitch slapped me

so i could catch

my falling senses.

i was losing respect

and

i was losing my way.

he said he had to

bitch slapped me

he said he had to

to bring back

the angel in me.

Cried-Out

she is crying

tears

but her well is

dry.

so, teardrops

aren't falling.

she has now become

immune to the lies.

how much more

can one woman

endure?

how much longer

is this going to last.

Lied-Out

she heard it
all before.

i will change,
just you wait and see.

it wouldn't happen again
baby.

please forgive me!

then it happened
again and again!

Daddy's Little Girl

what happened to
daddy's little girl?

what happened to
the angel of
daddy's eyes?

Crying Her Tears

i sat there and listened

to her story,

and i wonder:

how did she survive all these years?

how she managed to

smile so gracefully?

how she keeps her

effortless beauty?

now i'm left crying

her tears.

it's the daily burdens
she bears and
the unspeakable pains,

it's the thoughts about
what she has endured
i find hard to vocalise.

i see the pain in her eyes.
now i'm left crying
her tears.

He was My First

he popped
my sweet cherry.

he flipped my lid,
he gave me
my first taste of love.

he made me
groan with pleasure
and
screamed in pain.

he was my first

in so many ways.

now he is inflicting

daily pains.

He Gave Me a Child

the doctor said

it wasn't possible,

but

he made it possible.

have you seen

that child's eye?

he is my everything.

i have to make this work

just for him.

i love my baby boy.

he gave me a child

when they said

i couldn't have any.

i have to stay

and make this work.

he will change, i know

he will.

His Sugar Stick

he can make

the moon shines

ten times brighter

when he lays the

sugar stick on me.

is this reason enough to stay?

flowers bow at

the sound of his

whispering voice,

and

with one touch, my
juices flow effortlessly.

how can i leave this sweetness?

he has a magic stick
and with one wave,
i am paralyzed by love.

i would be a fool to leave this!

how can i leave?
why should i leave?

have you ever
tasted his sugar stick?
i didn't think so!

don't judge me!

Diary Insurance

(Just In Case)

just in case

i don't survive this,

my diary

will live to tell

my ghastly tale.

just in case

i'm too weak to speak

my diary

will be strong for me.

just in case

the scars are

no longer visible

my diary

will show the magnitude

of my hell.

just in case

no one believes me,

my diary

will show them

the unseen evidence.

please secure

my diary

it has been my

unconditional companion

and sense of hope

all these years.

Blood Love

it hurts,

but

i love him.

what do they know?

why should i

listen to them?

it hurts

but

i made a vow,

for better or

for worst.

it hurts

but

i will find a way

to make it work

i have to!

Only My Diary Knows

so many

untold stories.

so many

pearls of shattered tears.

so many

drops of blood.

so many

painful bruises.

only

my diary knows

the

actual stories,

only my dairy

knows the saltiness

of my tears

and the colour

of my smeared blood.

only my diary knows.

Runaway Love

i could hardly wait!

we were young
and
crazy in love.

so

i ignored
my parents' advice
and
joined the list of
runaway brides.

now in the midst
of all the pain
the idea is less
sexy and sweet.

what was i thinking?

now i'm isolated from my family
and taking a regular dose
of his unconscionable
beatings.

what was i thinking?

Before We Were Married

(He Uses to Be So Sweet)

he was my knight

in shining armour.

yes, he was!

my first love.

my cuddly bear.

my defender.

yes, he was!

then, in one

unsuspecting moment,

i tasted the wrath

of his anger and

the flavour

of my blood.

everything

changed from that moment

now our marriage

is not the same.

This Fucked-Up System

the judge said,
"give it one more try"
and
i believed in his
intellectual judgment.

the counsellor said,
*"together you can work it out
it's never too late"*
and
i decided to give it
another try,

AGAIN

hoping she was right

this time.

i was wrong!

the preacher said,

"take it to the lord

in prayer, get down

on your knees and pray,

repent and get baptised"

and i did.

but

after all this advice

i'm still in

the same shit!

the beatings

are flowing now

like showers of blessings,

should i say

thank you, lord?

The Carousel

it always starts off

with that

lovely, loving feeling.

we sync in so many ways

and in those areas where

we don't

we always find

workable compromises.

but once

the honeymoon phases

fades away and

my reality kicks in
things inevitably change.

some men run
instantaneously
others stick around
for a while
just to save face.

at the end of it all,
it seems like i am just
going through men
like a carousel.

my abusive past always
screw up
my relationships.

the reality is
none of them
seem to know
how to deal
with me during those
challenging times.

So,

here i am turning

this relationship carousel

once again.

who's next?

and how long will they last?

Exterior Glitters

you hear

the joyful laughter

but

you don't see

the depths of their pains.

you see

the intoxicating beauty

but you don't see

the gut-wrenching damages

that is beneath it all.

you don't see
the bruises,
you don't see
the blood that gushes
from battered veins.

you don't see
the bumps,
the black and blue patches.

you don't see what's hidden
beneath the makeup.

you hear about
the happy beginnings
but you don't hear about
the sad tales
that leave a trail
of psychological wounds
that refuse to heal.

you hear of the survivors' stories
but rarely do they tell you.
about those you never

survive the battering
to tell their harrowing tales.

this abusive relationship thing
is bigger than you know,
it's greater than they tell you,
it goes further back
than you expect,
it's deeper than
you can fathom.

it's sadder than
the joyous laughter,
it's wider than
the broad smile,
it's deeper than
my pensive thoughts.

my exterior appearance
is just a clown's mask
that hides
my wretched existence.

Her Story

my intuition told me
something was not right,

my experience calculator
in situations like this
was not adding up
the numbers correctly.

i respected her need
for privacy and
her need to heal,

but every so often i couldn't

resist the urge to probe
and prod and ask
some of the hard
uncomfortable questions.

then one day
out of the blues
she opened up
to me and told me
her story.

he was her first,
he broke her heart.
he gave her
a taste of true love
then he gave her reasons
to taste her blood.

he was privy
to her true beauty
and then he did everything
to tarnish it.

he kicked her
like a stray dog,

he locked her out
of their love nest,

he slept with someone else
in their marital bed.

many days he took her
to hell and back
and when she returned
he promises he would
never do it again.

but he did it.
again, and again
and again!

until she lost count
of how many trips
she made to that
forgettable place.

she has little or no
visible marks of violence,
her skin is almost spotless,
smooth as a baby's bottom

but the scars
in her heart,
it's too much
to take in all at once.

when she finally spoke,
from the heart,
i felt her pain.

i heard her silent tears,
my heart bled profusely
with every graphic detail.

she didn't cry then
because she had cried
so many times, before.

as i pen these words
i am crying the tears
she knew so well,

the tears burn
my drenched cheeks,
so deeply i wondered how
she survived it

for so long
all those years?

good look and good body
don't tell you
the authentic story.

i've learned that physical beauty
should never be the sole
barometer by which you
love and assess a woman.

some beautiful women
are burdened with some
of the darkest
and most damaged souls;
and as harsh as this sounds,
it's the brutal truth.

some of us men have lost
our moral core,
we don't know how
to truly love and respect
our women anymore.

Teardrops

when your teardrops

fall

do they make any sound?

when you cry

in the middle of

the night

does the darkness

cover your tears?

when you hurt in solitude

does that make you

feel stronger?

when the sadness

wells up inside

and

still, you smile

does it feel like a?

smiling a lie?

when you wipe away

your teardrops

does it get rid of the pains?

when you taste the saltiness

of your flowing tears

does it taste like honey?

when your teardrops

fall

do they make any sound?

The Sun Will Rise–Hope

come tomorrow,

the sun will rise

again

and bless you with

another opportunity

to

shine anew.

tomorrow

the sun will rise.

come tomorrow,

the sun will rise again

shining its light in those

dark places to guide

your way.

tomorrow

the sun will rise.

come tomorrow,

the sun will rise again

just for you,

shining love

unconditionally,

abundantly.

tomorrow

the sun will rise

come tomorrow,

the sun will rise again,

just for you.

Who?

who taught you
to smile
as a form of
hiding a lie?

who taught you
to say yes
when you should have
said no?

who told you
that your blessings were
worth nothing?

who made

you

feel less than

your true worth?

who told you

that you could

change him

by

changing you?

who taught you

to give all

your love

and looked for

nothing in return?

who told you

that you weren't beautiful

and

deserving of the best?

who told you

that you are

strong enough
to bear it all alone?

who told you
to never give up?

who and what are you listening to?

Wedding Vows

are wedding vows
unbreakable?

should you suffer
all these years
and
endure so many pains
because of your
wedding vows?

should wedding vows
come back to haunt

and

hurt you?

should they be remembered

every time you get

battered and bruised?

should you stay

for better

or for worst?

your wedding vows

are now rusted chains.

who is to take

the blame?

you or your wedding vows?

Running From Shadows

it doesn't matter
where i go i can feel them,
these long ghostly shadows
of my past.

nipping at my heels
in every new relationship,
whispering in my ears,
at the sight and sound
of love,

warning me to be
extra careful,

extremely vigilant,
and super protective
of the past hurts
and scars that i carry.

the long shadows
wouldn't let me be
they walk by me
and with me
wherever i go.

it doesn't matter
where i go i can feel them,
these long ghostly shadows
of my past calling me,

whispering my name,
driving me up the walls
of fear and insecurities.

Sweet Revenge

this revenged was served up
just the way the experts
prescribed it, COLD.

so why the hell
it feels so bitter
instead of sweet?

i found out
he was cheating
on me.

so i slept with a friend.

now i feel like
a piece of shit!

i feel empty,
i feel filthy,
i feel terrible.

so i confessed
my wrongdoings
to him because
i wanted to be
a better wife.

i thought that would
change things for us.

but it didn't.

it just got worse!
they say revenge
is a dish best served cold.

so why do i feel this way?

why did i follow
this dumb ass advice
in the first place?

now i am in deeper shit
than i was before.

damn,

i messed up big time!
i am such a fool!

Use to Be

when it all started
i use to make love.

foreplay and romancing
were my favourite things.

they made me sing
in tones and pitch
that would bring
my bedroom walls
to the ground.

these days
i just fuck
for the fun of it,

no need for those fineries.
no genuine feelings,
just a whole lot of faking it.

no attachments,
no real connections.

orgasms?
forget it, i don't know
what that is.

i never experienced it.

making love and
having passionate sex
use to be my thing.

these days,
i am just doing it,
for doing it sake.

i have mastered faking it!

HER DIARY EFFECT

The Opinionated Ones

Him

at this stage,

it should not be

about him.

this must be about you...

it's about you

taking back

your relinquished power.

it's about you

taking back

your self-esteem.

it's about you

taking back

your dignity.

it's about you

taking back

your inner beauty.

at this stage,

this should not be

about him.

this must be about you.

you

releasing your insecurities.

you

giving up your fears.

you

giving up

thoughts of weakness.

you

giving up your disbelief.

from here on

this should be about

you and you only.

Makeup and Mask

you have become adroit at
concealing the true reality.

makeup unfleek
so that all can admire,
a smiling mask
so that all perceived
your deceptive happiness.

how much more of
this charade
must your loved ones endure?

how long are you
going to cradle
the hurt in your bosom?

how much more of this
makeup and mask game
are you going to play?

What's so Special About Love?

why do some people
still, fall in love?

why do girls still fall
head over heels
at the sounds of these words?

why do i quiver
in fear whenever i hear them?

why some girls get weak in
the knees when that special

guy whispers those

magical words in their ears?

and why do i always feel

the need to run,

and not just run

but run far and fast

at the whispering of

those words?

hold on

sweet and innocent

baby girl,

hold up your macho buff,

don't be too quick

to judge me.

i spent years in a relationship

where my husband

said i love you

before he beat

the living daylight

out of me

he said, i love you
every time he beat me
to hell and back,

he said, i love you
while he took me forcefully,

he said, i love you while
i examine the destruction
in the mirror, he caused
to my face.

he said, i love you
while i struggled to see his face
out of the one good eye
i had left.

so don't be quick to
judge me
because i don't react
to i love you
the same way you do.

i have walked death's valley
hearing i love you,

i have been taken to hell's gate
hearing i love you,

i have been degraded
beyond recognition
hearing destructive words
coming from the same mouth
that said, i love you

so before you judge
just come walk a mile
in my "i love you" memories.

Behind Silent Fences

the world must never know!

you flood social media

with your happy pictures

and smiley faces

while

behind silent fences

you suffer severely.

the world must never see

your depressing side.

you have learned to adopt,

paint perfect pictures

of your imperfect and

sordid world.

skillful makeup jobs

hide bumps and bruises,

and there is very little that

overpower your fake smiles.

the world must never know

the pains and sorrows

you endure

behind your silent fences.

These Stories

left up to you,

these stories will

never be told.

i can talk about

your beauty

and

your natural sultriness

but

your hurting stories...

those don't exist.

left up to you,

these stories will

never be told.

i can talk about your

latest fashion statement

and

your pageant appearances

but

the stories that pain away

from the spotlight

must never be told.

left up to you,

these stories will

never be told.

i can talk about your

kindness and generosity

and

how you can always

people depend on it,

but the stories that shred

your heart to pieces

must never be told.

today,

i am telling your stories!

The Princess Who Became a Frog

you gave him

the best of

your youthfulness

and tender years,

but he didn't care.

he

wasn't prudent enough

to see your priceless gifts.

in his cruelty

and

insensitivity

he transformed you

from a princess

to a frog

and

you willing consented

in the name of love.

Your Daily Affirmations

you verbalize your reality
daily,
strengthening the mental
bars that keep you locked up.

"i'm not pretty enough for him
maybe that's the reason.

"i need to learn to cook better
so he will love me more."

"i need some more sexy clothing
and lingerie so i can be more
appeal for him."

"maybe i should bleach my skin
so i will be lighter and more attractive."

you verbalize
your perceived inadequacies
daily,

strengthening
the mental bars
that keeps you locked up
in your self-made prison.

Why Don't You Leave?

"why don't you leave?"

i ask

this question

from

the comfort of

my safe heaven

someone promptly educated me...

leaving isn't always that simple!

Breaking the Silence

silent no more!

i choose to speak up!

i choose to speak out!

it's no longer their business

in my selfish opinion.

it's no longer ok just

because it's not

my mother,□

my sister,□

my wife,□

my friend,□

or

my neighbour.

i'm telling you,□
don't stand by and judge
criticize and further victimized
do something.

break the cycle of silence.

abuse can only
thrive in silence.

shine the spotlight
on abuse by choosing to
speak up
and
speak out

today!

HER CLOSED DIARY

The Survivor Stories

A Healthy Relationship

sisters,□

please remember

a healthy relationship

will never make you feel

less than an individual.

a healthy relationship

will never ask you

to give up

your loved ones

and

trusted friends.

a healthy relationship

will never ask you

to sacrifice

your dreams,□

pride and dignity.

A Fortress Friend

when it gets

too much

to bear,□

a friend with a

listening ear

works wonders.

a friend with

sound advice,□

is a refreshing relief.

a friend who

refuses to support

your flimsy excuses

can go a long way

in helping you change.

A Place in Your Heart

your heart is sacred.

the spaces in

your heart must

reserve for

those who

made you a priority

in their life.

not for those who

made you an option.

safeguard those

spaces in your heart

for those who

make you feel

like the worthy person

you are.

Acknowledgement

you will be

challenged

to take many

steps

to your freedom.

you will be

challenged

to make many decisions

to change for

the better.

the greatest of

those challenges

will be

acknowledgement.

acknowledge

that you are hurting.

acknowledge

that it's unhealthy.

acknowledge

that you have to change.

acknowledge

that you have the strength

to do it.

acknowledge

that you are too

valuable to be devalued.

just acknowledge.

acknowledgement

is one of the

most important

steps towards recovery.

Be Proud

i don't think anyone can

understand

the strength it takes

to truly survive

any type of abuse.

when you love someone

deeply

who turns out to be

a monster

it's never easy.

you have survived.

be proud of yourself.

hold your head

high and smile with

all your might.

you deserve

this new found freedom.

Be Thankful

the days that follow

will not always be bright.

there will be

moments

of quiet

reflections

that burdens the soul.

there will be

images,□

smells,□

sounds

and

people who will

trigger

unpleasant memories.

learn gratitude.

be thankful.

give thanks for

what you have

at this moment.

but most important

be thankful for

what you have

survived and overcome.

Believe Them

when someone

treats you like

trash

when persons treat

like you are

not important,

when anyone treats

you like you are

less than human,

believe them.

when persons treat

you like you are not

important to them,

don't

question them,□

don't

doubt them,□

don't

try to make sense

of it.

believe them and

leave.

Break the silence

you must

break the silence,□

you must

smash silence into

a thousand pieces!

you must

believe in

speaking out,□

and

speaking up again.

your survival

depends on it,□

break the silence

give life to liberation.

Define

don't let

your experiences

define

who you are

today.

don't let

past hurt

define

the way you love

today.

don't let

yesterday's dirt

smear today's shine.

define today

on your terms.

How is it Possible

how can someone

who loves you

so deeply

yesterday,□

be so cruel

today?

how can someone

who makes you

feel like a queen

yesterday,

treats you

like

trash

today?

it hurts!

where is the logic?

don't try to comprehend

just get out!

before, it's□

too late.

I Made a Choice

i got tired.
tired of
the excuses,

tired of
the verbal
and
physical abuses.

tired of
subjecting myself
to something that
was

unhealthy for me

for too long.

so i made a choice,□

i chose to change.

i made up

my mind

from that day

i found the

inner strength

to move on,

implement

new solutions

to

old problems.

i set myself free

because i chose me.

Losing Your Love

we do so much

in the name

of love.

we give up

so much

for love.

we go through

so much

just to be loved.

but

losing yourself

just to love another

often

makes you forget

that you deserve

your love too.

don't lose

your self-love

while you are

too busy

loving someone else.

Loyalty

don't let

your loyalty becomes

your chains.

don't let

your need

for commitment

be the bars that

imprison you.

don't be so blind

that

your loyalty

becomes

your enslaver.

No Surrender

they can assault
your pride

they may batter
your dignity

they may dull
your shine,

but

they can never
conquer
or

dominate you

unless you surrender.

never surrender!

stand firm,□

stand strong,□

it's built into your dna.

Over You

i have a new outlook
on life,

i have a new lease
on living,

i have so much more
love in me
still to give.

i'm so much
more than
you told me i was.

i am

happily living

life anew.

i'm, over you. □

Perish the Thoughts

pesky and persistent,

curiously cunning,

these

haunting thoughts

refuse to die.

disrupters of

peace of mind,

polluters of purity,

these memories

of yesterday

will not go away.

perish the thoughts of...

what if?

how come?

why me?

will i make it?

who will love me?

perish these

unhealthy thoughts,□

they are killers

of your

peace of mind.

Psychological Invalidation

it's the dagger

that pierces

you

emotionally.

it kills your will

to go on.

it stifles

your creative instincts.

psychological invalidation

destroys

your individuality

in a jiffy.

safeguard yourself at

all times.

Refreshing Realisations

i sit here with a
satisfying smile
on my face,

because i'm staring
to remember
the real me.

the one i forgot
after years of thinking...
i was not worthy.

worthy

of better,

worthy

of love,

worthy

of happiness,

worthy

of peace of mind.

i'm falling in love

with this

refreshing thoughts...

i'm worthy.

Sacrifice Your Heart

there is too much

at stake.

too much

to lose.

too much

to destroy.

it's better to

break your own heart

just once,

than have

your heart

broken daily

by their

insensitivity

and

insecurity.

sacrifice

your heart

for your

greater good.

Self-Value

despite what

they say

it doesn't get better

if you don't

take a stand.

be your own friend,

have compassion

for yourself,

learn to forgive

you.

know your true value,□

demand

that you are

treated

with respect.

never ever

give up.

you will

survive and overcome.

Shadows for a Lifetime

the hurt can
sometimes cast
dark shadows
that's long enough
to last a lifetime.

be patient
with yourself
as you heal.

recovery is not a
one day process,

it's takes

daily work

and

deliberate commitment.

love yourself

through the process.

you spent

a long time

in a dark place,

it will take

some time to adjust

to the bright and

refreshing light of healing.

love yourself

through the recovery.

Silence

silence in

abusive relationship

is dangerous.

silence is

an enabler.

silence

can be a killer.

speak up!

speak out!

speak,□

your survival depends on it.

Silent Suffering

too often we see silence

as a lack of courage

to reach out

or

the inability to cry out

for help.

but what is seldom known

and less seen

is the many occasions

when you

reach out,□

speak out, and□

they scorn your pleas,□

and

victimise you even more.

sometimes

suffering in silence

is the lesser

of two devils.

when you have been

hurt so often,□

every time

you reach out

for help,

suffering in silence

becomes more comforting.

Some Scars

some scars

no longer hurt.

some scars

render you insensitive.

some scars

makes you paranoid.

some scars

empower you.

some scars

make you numb.

but despite

the scars,□

life can still

be beautiful.

you must remember to live

each moment like

it's a precious gift.

Someday

don't give up.
don't give in.

someday
you find that
elusive strength
to stand up and
fight for you.

to
stand up and
walk away.

someday

you will find

strength

you never thought

you had.

Survivor Story

not everyone will

understand,☐

not everyone will

empathise,☐

not everyone will

believe.

some will trivialise

your experiences,☐

some will turn

a blind eye.

other will be

indifferent.

write your reality,□

share your experiences,□

be the voice

for the voiceless.

you are free now,□

be the whistleblower

for the silent suffers.

don't let the

lack of understanding

by others

deny you and

someone who could be

encouraged by your survivor story.

The Aftermath

it's not the

bruises and bumps

on the body that

hurts the most.

it's the wounds inflicted

on the heart

that extends to

the mind

and the haunting

reminders.

it's the

little things

that often hurts

the most.

after survival,□

some memories

still loiter,

but

continue

to live

continue

to heal.

The Love Factor

i have come

to learn a

slow and painful

fact.

some persons aren't

worth having

in my life.

despite how much

i love them,□

despite how strong

my feelings.

i'm better without

them in my life.

sometimes

loving someone

is not a

strong enough

reason to stay.

The Mental Battles

the mental battles

are still

ever-present.

you find yourself

fighting so often

with someone

you no longer have

any contact with.

the small voices,

recurring memories,

unpleasant feelings.

they just don't

disappear

but never give up,

never give in,□

this too

you shall win.

There is Always a Way

sometimes it seems

like there is

no way out,

no silver lining behind

the darkest of clouds.

your head droops,

your confidence wilts,

your will to go on

it is being sucked dry.

snap out of that mindset!

there is always

a way out.

always!

there is always

someone

who is willing and

able to help.

there is always a way

when you have

the desire to heal, and☐

move on,

always!

To Hell and Back

i have stared
death in the face,

run down
the streets of hell
screaming.

i lay with the devil,
slept with the enemy.

dined with danger
and despite that,

i live to

tell the tales.

i have survived!

now i shine

brighter than the sun,□

i'm fresher than the

morning dew.

i can live without you!

i made it because

i refused to allow

you

to destroy my femininity,□

watch me burgeon.

Truth Illusions

as you walk

the path

to recovery

many things will be

apparent.

old facts

become opinions.

archaic beliefs

reveal themselves.

so-called truths

turn out to

be fancy lies.

some traditions

cherished become burdens.

friendly smiles

show there

deceitful sides.

some truths were

nothing but

an illusion.

Unappreciated

you can spend

years in situations

where you are

unappreciated.

venomous relationships

has the power

to alter your

perception of reality.

you can easily believe

that

you are worthless.

just because you are

unappreciated by someone

doesn't mean

you are worthless,

it just means

you are not

appreciated by

that person.

Walk Away

staying and fight

for an

unhealthy relationship

is not noble.

despite what they

tell you

it is not brave.

fighting for someone

who continues to

break you

is not prudent.

walk away!

walk

away!

walk... away

it's the bravest thing

you can do.

walk.

just walk away.

Wandering Mind

control your thoughts.

guard the gates
of your mind.

sometimes
your wandering mind
can take you back
to unhealthy places
you left behind.

sometimes
your wandering mind

can destroy all

the present gains.

control your

wandering mind.

Wear them with Pride

every scar tells
a story.

every wound tells
of unspeakable pain.

wear them as
a badge of honour.

you have survived
despite the odds
against you,

despite everyone else

giving up on you.

you have survived!

and

your scars and wounds

will always tell

your story.

a story of strength

and resilience.

a survivor story.

When Sorry Means Nothing

when sorry becomes

a pattern

and

lose

its true meaning

leave...

leave,□

quickly!

When Good Goes Bad

change happens,□
sometimes it's fast

sometimes it's slow,□
but there are
always signs.

don't ignore them
don't make excuses.

when the good
turns to bad
and remains bad.

leave.

run.

move.

whatever you do
don't stay!

don't wait to
seek help,

don't wait to
get out

don't wait!

just leave.

You Can Do It!

i know it doesn't

seems so now,□

but

you can do it.

you can take the

first step.

you can get out.

you can get help.

you can

speak to someone.

you can survive

without him.

you can move on,☐

you can find

love again.

You Deserve Better

believe in yourself

and

remind yourself

that you

deserve better.

You Will Survive

the road to

recovery

may be long

but

you will make it.

after all,□

you have survived

the abuse,□

you were strong enough

to leave.

R. A. BENTINCK

you have

what it takes

to recover fully.

About the Author

r. A. bentinck

r. A. bentinck is a poet, artist, educator, and storyteller whose work traces the delicate line between memory and emotion, truth and silence. With over three decades of experience teaching across Guyana and the Caribbean,

Bentinck has spent a lifetime listening, really listening, to the quiet confessions, private fears, and unguarded moments that reveal the human heart.

His writing blends poetic precision with emotional honesty, shaped by years of supporting women who trusted him with their unspoken stories. As a marathon runner and lifelong creative, Bentinck brings discipline, empathy, and a deep respect for resilience to every page he crafts.

His poetry explores the hidden landscapes of love, trauma, identity, and survival, inviting readers to pause, breathe, and confront the truths many are taught to hide. With a voice rooted in Caribbean sensitivity and universal understanding, Bentinck creates work that makes readers feel both seen and strengthened.

Underneath the Poetry with Her Diary stands as one of his most intimate and courageous offerings, a tribute to the women whose whispered truths deserved a witness, and to every reader searching for words powerful enough to hold their own story.

* 9 7 8 0 9 9 9 9 4 4 4 5 2 8 *